LUST[

GW00759543

Lustleigh, without doubt, is my favourite D   hose who share the same sentiment and enthusiasm and who want to know a .....   jewel of Eastern Dartmoor set in its glorious surrounding countryside.

In the mid nineteenth century Samuel Rowe visited the village and noted the attributes of this cosy place: *"Lustleigh Church is placed on the pleasant slope of one of our deepest Devonshire coombs, where the most pleasing features of village scenery are combined, whilst not a single uncongenial object intrudes to mar the keeping of the harmonious whole. A clear vigorous*

stream, ripples cheerily down the dell – to turn the busy mill at the end of the hamlet; graceful shelving acclivities partitioned by varied foliage in green crofts, or blooming garden grounds, substantial farmsteads, and whitewashed cottages, peep from among the orchards, or are nestled under sheltering trees. Boulder rocks, with thicket and copse interspersed, protrude from the soil,

on the higher ground, while the far-famed Lustleigh Cleave with its granite barrier, fences in the vale from the storms of the neighbouring moor. The combination of rural scenery of this particular class, thus presented in this seques- tered spot is certainly not surpassed, if equalled, in any other part of Devonshire."

Those 'boulder rocks' are a feature of the Lustleigh district and there are many scattered around the parish. Some, with overhangs, can be a godsend. When I was doing the 'hands-on' bit (i.e. on foot!) of researching this book, I was glad of the shelter afforded by one of these rocks. High above Hammerslake, I took refuge whilst a hailstorm sent down a battery of ear-stinging hailstones, some the size of marbles! Such is the changeable nature of Dartmoor weather that just a few minutes later the sun was shining.

Another writer of the past, Page, described Lustleigh as he saw it: *"With its houses dotted irregularly on the slopes, it looks as if it had been dropped from the skies."* The famous Dartmoor author, William Crossing, who died in 1928, mirrored this observation: *"Lustleigh is small but has a pleasing appearance, not only on account of its delightful situation, but for the manner in which the cottages are dotted about."*

Certainly there is a pleasing, random look about the village when seen from the surrounding hillsides.

The fame and beauty of Lustleigh have spread far and wide. A Belgian photographic agency brought a top female model to the village. Here she went through many costume changes and struck a variety of poses around the village. Henry Tudor's memorial cross, near the church, has rarely had so much attention! These various 'visual representations' may account for why some visitors experience that feeling of *déjà-vu* when they first arrive.

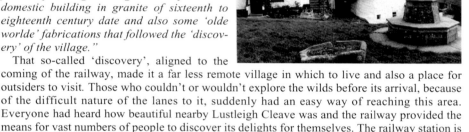

The late Professor W. G. Hoskins, a celebrated and much-quoted historian, visited Lustleigh many times. He described it as: *"... a picturesque village with a good deal of excellent domestic building in granite of sixteenth to eighteenth century date and also some 'olde worlde' fabrications that followed the 'discovery' of the village."*

That so-called 'discovery', aligned to the coming of the railway, made it a far less remote village in which to live and also a place for outsiders to visit. Those who couldn't or wouldn't explore the wilds before its arrival, because of the difficult nature of the lanes to it, suddenly had an easy way of reaching this area. Everyone had heard how beautiful nearby Lustleigh Cleave was and the railway provided the means for vast numbers of people to discover its delights for themselves. The railway station is now a private dwelling but if it could talk it could tell of film crews shooting here, and members of the Royal Family coming and going and also name-drop a host of other famous visitors.

In those glorious years of steam trains this was a lively place. There was even a station cat, Jumbo, who, having used his full quota of nine lives was finally laid to rest on the platform. His epitaph was simple: *"Beneath this slab, and laid out flat, lies Jumbo, once our station cat."* Unfortunately there is no trace of it today, so it's only in the realms of literature that it survives as a piece of railway folklore.

The station used to possess a visitors' book which was the subject of an article by 'WGC' in the GWR magazine of July 1923, when the railway was at its peak of popularity. *"To the station master at Lustleigh, Mr F. J. Haywood, is due the credit for having introduced a book in the station waiting room for the reception of views and opinions of visitors respecting the attractions of this beauty spot in the 'Shire of the Sea kings'. The idea is a happy one which might with advantage be followed at other places.*

Started in 1916, the book contains the tributes of visitors from far and near, e.g. Canada, Jamaica and Nigeria, besides a host of testimonies from numerous English holidaymakers who flocked to the West of England for their vacations during the time when air raids were not unknown elsewhere in our country.

The wealth of praise of the beauties of Lustleigh's surroundings contained between the covers of this volume would do credit to the most eulogistic verbosity of a guide-book writer, and it is doubtful if any adjective suggesting the 'delectable,' 'exquisite,' 'beautiful' or 'picturesque' has been omitted. Whilst not a few of the writings are in humorous vein and some border on the cynical, the general effect is a record of genuine appreciation of the unique charms of this 'Corner of God's Garden,' as one visitor describes it.

In one instance, a testimony to the natural beauty of the locality is linked with a request for more 'houses of public refreshment,' and another shows the mixed mentality of the writer who, after exhausting his vocabulary in praise of Nature's handiwork, suggests, if you please, that a 'good picture show' would be a desirable acquisition.

There are, of course, frequent references to The Cleave, Becky Falls, the Bullaton and Nutcracker Rocks; and 'the old Cottage' comes in for its measure of admiration. These laudations are, however, not entirely limited to the scenery, for visitors to Lustleigh also bear written tribute of their appreciation of the station, the station garden, and the station staff ... Here is variety, for whilst the following is contributed by a visitor from California, USA., 'Beautiful Devon! Home of our ancestors. Almost equal to our Southern California, USA,' on the next page we have an admission from a Swansea visitor that 'Lustleigh is a lot better than Landore.' ...

One visitor who goes into ecstasies over the old cottage, and the rustic bridge built in 1680, concludes with: 'A lovely cream tea at Mrs Ellis's cannot be beaten.'

As evidence ... one writer records the fact of having visited Lustleigh every year since 1872, and is coming again next year. What higher testimony is needed?"

A headline which appeared in the local press, along with this picture, posed the question "What railway station is this?" Although there wasn't an accompanying article we know it's Lustleigh because the word Baskerville is a giveaway. Scenes from the film *Hound of the Baskervilles* were shot here in March 1931. More than half a century later another film version of the same story, which starred Martin Shaw and Ian Richardson, was also partly filmed in the district.

This railway was a branch line which ran from Newton Abbot across the Bovey Basin, before following the Bovey and the Wray valleys up to Moretonhampstead, the railhead, at a much higher elevation. The Wray valley is part of a geological fault-line known as the 'Sticklepath Fault', which straddles the county. It is a stunningly beautiful valley and there are some excellent footpaths in and around it. The main road follows the valley and it's one which needs to be driven with a great deal of care. The former railway would have provided a less stressful corridor through this countryside.

If you want to hear some unusual anecdotes and read much more of the history of this branch line then you should read another of my books, *Railways on and around Dartmoor*.

But not everyone who has written about Lustleigh has seen the village through rose-tinted spectacles. One of my former lecturers, and brilliant writer of many books about Devonshire topics, S. H. Burton, had this to say in his book *Devon Villages*, published in 1973, which pulled no punches: *"... property in the village fetches exorbitant prices and few true villagers remain. Ex-Forces and upper-class retired dominate the place. Soon, you will have to be very well off indeed to live in Lustleigh. This is symptomatic, of course, of the 'Devon Disease'. It was – and is (if one can revalue its function) – a charming village."*

The village of Lustleigh is clustered around its lovely church of St John the Baptist, a building which has played an important part in the life of this community for centuries.

The church has had some colourful clerics. The Rev William Davy, B.A., who was for nearly 40 years curate in charge of the parish, was one of them. The Rev Thomas Moore wrote this of him many years ago: *"Whilst at college he formed the idea of compiling a complete System of Divinity, selected from the most approved and orthodox divines, both ancient and modern. In the year 1786, he published by subscription, six volumes of sermons, by way of introduction to his intended work; but this proved an unfortunate speculation, many of the subscribers forgetting to pay for their copies, and he remained in consequence indebted to his printer above £100. This bad success, however, did not discourage him; he pursued his researches, and completed the work; but when completed the estimated cost of publication was £2,000. He again contemplated publication by subscription ... but the names collected were too few. Not willing to be deprived of the honour of authorship he determined to turn printer himself and in pursuance of this purchased a font of worn-out type from Messrs Trewman, of Exeter. Now his mechanical genius*

(for which he had been remarkable as a boy) served him and he set himself up to make a printing press ... In this manner did this ingenious and persevering man, sustained by the hope of doing good, and the anticipation of literary bays, proceed until he had printed off forty copies of the first 300 pages – his press allowing him to only work off one page at a time. Imagining he had now produced an ample specimen ... he forwarded 26 copies to the various universities, and the Royal Society, to the bishops, and the editors of the principal reviews, and for a while rested from his labours, and waited anxiously for that notice and assistance he conceived himself of receiving from those quarters. He waited in vain – the encouragement came not. Again disappointed he became even more determined ... [and] completed the remaining fourteen copies. He had, at last, after thirteen years of unremitting toil, the gratification of

bringing his extraordinary task to a conclusion. His labour and patience need not be dwelt upon; it will be readily admitted he possessed the most patient industry ... "

Another article affirmed his enthusiasm but reinforced the sort of attitude which he encountered in his quest for acknowledgment: *"Mr Davy presented a copy to his diocesan, Dr Fisher, for the Cathedral library of St Peter, Exeter, where it may now be seen. On his presenting the copy, his Lordship remarked that he could not be supposed to notice every trifle that appeared in print.*

'Well, my Lord, if you consider 26 volumes, the labour of 50 years in collecting, compiling, and printing a trifle, I certainly cannot allow myself to expect from your Lordship either encouragement or support.' Like others who have gone before him he found that talent and piety are too often sacrificed at the shrines of favouritism and worldly influence.

In December 1825, at the age of 83. he was presented by the Bishop of Exeter to the vicarage at Winkleigh, Devon. He was gratified at this token of remembrance but his sand was nearly exhausted. He performed the duties of his church but after a few Sundays – the fatigue and excitement of the change accelerated a disease under which he had long been suffering, and terminated his life of anxiety and disappointment on June 12th, 1836 [sic]. *Lieut Worthy in his History of the Manor and Church of Winkleigh states that 'he was buried, at his own request, in the chancel of his church; and his grave-stone has an inscription recording his literary labours, and also stating that "his zeal and labour in the work of his calling were great, persevering and successful."' Mr Davy is said to have laid out his garden at Lustleigh in shrubs, in the shape of the Lord's Prayer, and the Ten Commandments."*

He was accompanied, in producing his monumental printing job, by his dedicated servant Mary Hole. The Rev William Davy (1743–1826) was quite a man, the sort who obviously refused to take 'No' for an answer. He also published some 500 of his sermons and was therefore obviously a man of words. Had the Rev Davy had today's technology his task would have been easier. However, in a very different world his 'System of Divinity' would also probably have been a very different one too!

Another Lustleigh man was the Victorian actor, the one and only Nutcombe Gould. This brief obituary appeared in the press in 1899: *"The late Mr Nutcombe Gould, who was laid to rest in the little cemetery at Lustleigh on Saturday, was an actor of great promise who was just on the eve of obtaining that recognition by players and playgoers alike, which would have given him a high position on the stage. His last provincial tour as leading man with Mr Patrick Cambell, revealed in him a talent for character-acting of which he had not been suspected, and his fine impersonation of the infirm and passionate Schwartze in 'Magda' was a piece of acting of which Adolf Klein himself might have been proud. Scarcely less noteworthy was his appearance as Aubrey Tanqueray in Mr Pinero's play – a character in which he exhibited all those traits of a dignified English gentleman which characterised his own private and public life."*

James Nutcombe Gould's (1849–1899) low headstone is close to the main entrance and is shared by Edith Gould (1859–1900). There is a lovely lantern on the wall almost beside his headstone. It was restored in 1994 to the memory of Philip St Leger Attenborough (1908–1991) by his wife Kathleen and his family. If you think Nutcombe is an unusual Christian name, spare a thought for the Rev Nutcombe Nutcombe. This man of the cloth died, aged 83, on 22 November 1809 and is featured on a memorial stone at Exeter Cathedral.

In the church is a memorial to Colonel Amery (1873–1955), statesman and mountaineer, who achieved much in his life as the inscription reveals. In the late 1920s he was given a warm home-coming by the local Liberals and Unionists. The report of this occasion included the following: *"Members of the Amery family had been prominent in history of England but none excelled the success of their illustrious guest ... Colonel Amery said that although born*

in India he spent his happiest days in Lustleigh where, as a boy, he spent his holidays. The Amery clan had their headquarters in Lustleigh for two or three centuries, but he found family members all over the world. Although they all developed a local patriotism they all remembered Devon with affection ... He not infrequently came down to Lustleigh himself, to wander alone or with his friend, Mr Amery, of Ashburton but this was the first time he had come into contact with Lustleigh people and with many members of the family that still resided there and in the district.

Mr C. D. Bennett proposed a vote of thanks and said they were proud that a Lustleigh boy had won his way to the Cabinet. They were all glad that he had not lost 'the Lustleigh pull'. He later visited the former family home, Middle Combe, and spent the afternoon walking the district." Leopold Stennett Amery's headstone, in the churchyard, tells us that his ashes are buried here, as is his wife Florence (1881–1975).

In the graveyard of this church, where his forbears worshipped through many generations, lie the ashes of

LEOPOLD STENNETT AMERY

PRIVY COUNCILLOR · COMPANION OF HONOUR
FELLOW OF ALL SOULS
Born in India 1873   Died in London 1955

As Times Correspondent, Author, Member of Parliament for Birmingham, First Lord of the Admiralty, Secretary-of-State for Dominions and Colonies, Secretary-of-State for India and Burma, he devoted his life in Peace & War to the service of the British Commonwealth and Empire

On his death, Sir Winston Churchill said:

"I mourn the loss of my friend Leo Amery. Statesman and man of letters, he was above all a great patriot."

This tablet was erected by his wife and surviving son

There is a legend attached to Lustleigh's church, a variation of one which is found at other places of worship in the county. A man enters this House of God carrying a pack of cards in his pocket and, by magic, Satan appears. The Devil threatens to fly off with the man unless a suitable sacrifice is quickly offered up. A friend of the man races from the church and sees a poor innocent moggy in the churchyard so grabs the frightened feline and offers her up to Satan who, easily placated, gleefully accepts the alternative offering. Poor puss! With his quarry stashed beneath his black cloak, the Devil rides out to an accompaniment of blue fire and brimstone! Stories like this would have made most people behave themselves when entering church and forced them to sit through some tediously long and mind-numbingly boring sermons!

A former schoolhouse stands in the churchyard and dates back to 1825, when discipline was tough and the curriculum narrower than the lanes leading to Lustleigh.

The steps leading up to the lich gate, at the entrance to the church, were placed in 1887 to commemorate the Golden Jubilee of Queen Victoria.

Although it's wonderful to live in a 'roses-round-the-door' cottage, or even in a small mansion,

it's not always as idyllic or romantic as the poets would have it. This article, from 1932, illustrates the other side of the stark realities of life when things go wrong:

"An old English mansion, of the type that Americans would give vast sums to transplant to their own country, was wholly ruined by fire at Lustleigh last night. The scene of the outbreak was Yonder Wreyland, a beautiful thatched roof country house, which was once the home of the late Mr Cecil Torr.

Yonder Wreyland was in the occupation of Miss Greer as a guest-house. As a result of the outbreak about 20 people were rendered homeless, and last night found shelter in various houses and cottages in the village. There was a great fear when the fire was at its height that a large number of cottages in the immediate vicinity might become involved.

'It might have led to the most disastrous conflagration that Mid-Devon has known for many years,' said the chief officer of Bovey Fire Brigade (Mr L. S. Mardon) observed when he paused for a moment in his duties ... The fire originated in a corner of the thatched roof ... The strong wind fanned the flames into a great fury ... Fortunately there was a plentiful supply of water but nothing could save the burning house.

Before the arrival of the fire brigade most of the furniture had been removed, including paintings stated to be of considerable value ... The property was owned by Mr E. Carritt of Oxford, and was insured.

'It was a real show place and a thing of beauty,' said a resident ... 'It was one of the very old manors standing' he added."

However, one reader was misled by the report and wrote this to the press: "The fire at Yonder Wreyland on Wednesday night destroyed not only a beautiful building, but one which had obtained wide celebrity through the literary labours of its former owner, the late Cecil Torr. His three volumes of Small Talk at Wreyland, made the house and its surroundings familiar to thousands who had never seen it, and who now will have no opportunity of becoming acquainted with it, except as a ruin or possibly a modern reconstruction on the old lines. The fact that the fire originated in the thatched roof lends pathetic interest to what its former proud owner had to say on this mode of covering buildings. Thatch, in Mr Torr's opinion, was the ideal roofing, warm in winter and cool in summer, and no one who had lived in a thatched house would, he said, willingly live under any other. As to the fire risks, though insurance companies charged higher rates, he was convinced that thatch was not really inflammable. It would only burn slowly, like a book, and fire could be stopped by cutting away a strip and making a gap that the fire could not cross. Unfortunately this did not prove to be the case on this occasion, and it was only by mere luck that the whole hamlet was not destroyed."

Unfortunately he had mistakenly thought that it was Wreyland Manor, shown here, which had been destroyed. His written apology read: "Sir,– I appear before you this·morning as a penitent. Seven times I bow before you and bewail the incorrectness of the letter of mine which you were so kind to print on Saturday last."

May Day has, for a great many years, been an important date on the Lustleigh calendar. Television presenter David Young made a series of short films about villages throughout the West Country. In the subsequent book, called An A to Z of Villages, his letter 'L' was Lustleigh. This is what he had to say of the May Day celebrations: "Lustleigh is one of those villages that was fortunate to survive the Great Plague that swept the country during the fourteenth century mainly because it was surrounded by a river and the rodents could not get across. To celebrate their good fortune the villagers decided that every year on May Day they would have a festival and elect a Queen. The Queen's throne is in the Orchard and carved on that throne are the names of all the May Day Queens since 1954.

Apparently things do not always run smoothly on May Day. One former Queen recounted to me how at her ceremony a goat broke loose and started eating all the flowers adorning her throne; before he could be stopped he started on the canopy of flowers! The children were singing well but they could not be heard because the crowd was laughing so much."

The ceremony has not always been held in the Orchard. Here is another report, this time from 1939: *"Bedecked with gay flowers and chanting tunefully the roundelays and songs associated for ages with May Day celebrations, children of Lustleigh, near Newton Abbot, yesterday crowned their Queen of the May, for whom a large granite boulder made a throne for a day.*

The May Queen was Miss Phyllis Wills. The ritual followed the precedent established through the centuries, but to the children, garlanded with roses, tulips, primroses, lilac, and other flowers, it might never have been performed at any other time, to judge from the freshness and pleasure shown in performance.

Spick and span in their white dresses and carrying colourful posies of flowers, none had in mind the keen wind and the grey skies.

Before the crowning ceremony the May Queen and her train marched through the village streets, where thatched roof dwellings still predominate.

A canopy of floral decorations was held above her by bearers, and at her side walked the 'Archbishop' (Arthur Horrell) and the 'Sceptre Bearer' (John Dray), who carried a beautiful lily.

Behind came twelve trim Maids of Honour and the Maypole dancers.

On the steps of the parish church and in other spots the children sang May Day songs, and then climbed the long ascent to Long Tor, overlooking a vast expanse of Devon, where the floral crown was set in place by the 'Archbishop' and where the name of one more Lustleigh May Queen has been inscribed on a granite rock set aside for that purpose.

Amid songs, posies of flowers were set at the feet of the 'Queen,' and Maypole dancing followed."

The 1917 celebrations were at a time of war and there was a shortage of cereals which threatened the success of the tea. However, the influential and extremely kind-hearted Cecil Torr stepped in to rescue the situation by providing some two hundred hard-boiled eggs.

The May Day celebrations were decidedly muted in 1927. It was reported widely in the press that: *"The news of the Rector's death was received just prior to the commencement of the May Day celebrations, which have been carried on without a break for 23 years. Consequently, the programme was curtailed ... Following the ceremony Maypole dances were given by the children to the strains of the Bovey Tracey band. Through the kindness of Mr Cecil Torr, of Wreyland, who bears the expense of the proceedings, the children were entertained to tea, and the May Queen was presented with a butterfly-wing pendant, suspended on a silver-necklace ..."*

The *Devon & Exeter Gazette*, a few days later, reported that: *"Amid many indications of sympathy and respect, the interment took place in Lustleigh parish churchyard yesterday of the Rev H. B. Martin (Rector), whose death occurred on Monday after a long illness. The day had been chosen for the May Day celebrations in the village, and the May Queen's crown was placed with the family's tribute on the coffin."* The Rev Henry Basil Martin had held office for less than twelve months but his passing was much lamented.

Today the May Day festivities take place on the first Saturday in May. This colourful event still draws large crowds and still presents that freshness commented on so enthusiastically all those years ago. Cecil Torr would certainly appreciate the villagers' efforts to keep the tradition, which he rekindled in 1904, still going.

Around & About Lustleigh

The Town Orchard, a wonderful sanctuary for peace and quiet, was given by Mrs M. E. Bennett, to the village, in March 1966 and there is a stone to commemorate this act of benevolence placed on the well-worn path between the entrance and the May Day Rock. The aptly-named Orchard Garage is near that entrance and next to the all-important public conveniences.

Lustleigh may be a small village but it has its excellent Stable House Gallery, which draws people in from afar with its arts, crafts, ornaments, gifts and local books. It's believed that its name is corrupted from 'staple' either by dint of a spelling mistake or a slip of the pen. Nearby Moretonhampstead was heavily involved in the woollen industry, so as 'staple' was a technical term for a fibre of wool it's possible that a branch of that cottage industry was located here. It could also be because 'staple' meant the centre of the community and as this building is located close to the church this may also be a possible meaning. As this old picture postcard shows, it was once the post office and run by the Bibbings family.

Primrose Cottage, the village's famous award-winning tea-room, the subject of numerous national and international articles, has only been there since 1948. The site has seen other uses and the village's former petrol station, possibly a one pump affair, was here at one time.

There is also the Post Office, a focal point of activity and, opposite, the Dairy which is now a grocery shop owned by 'shareholders', many of them local people, who effectively guarantee its survival.

In the past there were more shops as Lustleigh had a greater degree of independence. One of the businesses to survive almost a century before being forced out of business was the Brookfield Bakery. It began in the 1880s and developed after the First World War, when deliveries were made in a Bull-nose Morris van. For years Lustleigh villagers could enjoy the wonderful smell of fresh bread, but the competition from the growth of supermarkets proved to be too fierce and the bakery ceased operation after 98 years of family trading.

The Cleave is a whitewashed fifteenth-century longhouse. It was originally the farmhouse of the village's main farm, known as 'Gatehouse', but it also had religious connections. Part of it was

used by monks of Buckfast Abbey as a place of prayer when they visited the village. It became a hotel in the 1920s and then an inn. In an age when landlords, and landladies, often come and go with alarming regularity, it's even more impressive to note that for more than forty years Mrs Scott Painter was at the Cleave Hotel.

The Old School House's name is a giveaway as to its former function. It was built in 1870 and Lustleigh children, for several generations, went to school there. Many recall a former head teacher, Mr Collier, who was as tough as nails but fair. During the years of the Second World War pupils were encouraged to take an egg to school with them for lunch, this diet being supplemented by a mug of hot cocoa. The school closed in 1963 and from that time on village children could attend schools at Moretonhampstead or Bovey Tracey. Although the school bell remained at Lustleigh the clock was parcelled up and shipped to Australia.

In a village as small as Lustleigh every monument counts towards its history and heritage; the war memorial is one of them. On it are carved the names of those 'gallant men of Lustleigh' who made the ultimate sacrifice. The opening ceremony was a moving occasion for those who lost loved ones. Here are a few snippets from the report of the unveiling ceremony: *"Several years have passed since the greatest war in the history of the world came to an end, and perhaps the memory of those who gave their lives ... But a few days since the villagers of Lustleigh, showed*

that their appreciation of fallen parishioners has been unaffected by the flight of time. A memorial to them was unveiled by General Sir Alexander J. Godley G.C.B., K.C.M.G ... and dedicated by the Bishop of Exeter. It is one of which any place the size of Lustleigh could feel justly proud ... The stone of which it is composed is grey Devonshire granite. The central figure is a weather-worn boulder, with a cross graven upon it. Steps lead up from the road level ... Under the boulder is an airtight receptacle containing a roll of the names of all men and women of the parish who served in the war. The memorial is believed to be the only one in England, so far as can be ascertained, that has been erected entirely under the auspices of a local branch of the British Legion. The site was given by Major-General W. J. Fawcett and the design and working drawings were made by Col. A. S. Dunlop who also supervised the construction ...*

The unveiling and dedication were performed in the presence of a large gathering in typical spring weather ... Sir Alexander Godley unveiled the memorial by pulling aside two small flags that covered the name panels, and a large Union Jack that obscured the boulder ... " There were hymns sung, speeches made and a great feeling of local pride. A schoolboy was the janitor and held a badge of office.

The Teign Naturalists' Field Club was a very active organisation in the early twentieth century. Lustleigh was the subject of their attention on 20 May 1905, when their monthly meeting saw them visit the village to further their knowledge. This is just part of the report, by A. J. Davy, that covered their visit to this moorland-edge parish.

"Of the many thousands of residents and visitors who go from Torquay to Lustleigh every year, one wonders how many of them have noted the Bishop's Stone in the hedge near the railway station, or the curious inscribed stone at the entrance to the parish church, both objects of great interest and antiquity ... At the request of the Hon Sec (Colonel Amery), I prepared and read the following paper, the details of which were gathered from various sources ...

I read as follows: By the roadside is a singular relic called 'the Bishop's Stone,' to which the gossips of the parish have attached many an idle tale. This block of grey granite is fixed in the hedge near the four cross-ways. It has carefully been wrought into octagon-shape, and in front is a shield displaying the arms of the See, impaling those of Bishop Cotton who presided over the diocese from 1597 to 1621. At the back of the stone are the initial letters T.C. Various are the conjectures as to the object of the stone. There appears every reason to believe it was intended for preaching, and placed there, very probably, by Thomas Comyn, who was instituted to the Rectory of Lustleigh by Bishop Cotton in 1607; and it is natural to imagine that he may have been desirous of marking the period of erection, by placing the arms of his diocesan in front, and T.C. at the back, being his own initials.

Some have supposed that it was the pedestal of a cross, but this is very improbable, as the top is perfectly smooth, whilst another conjecture is that of an early practice of erecting stones of this kind at the meeting of three or four roads, and not far distant from a church. At these crosses a corpse being carried to church was set down, that all people who attended might pray for the soul of the departed. A tradition prevails that the arms were those of Bishop Grandisson, who once passed through Lustleigh, and dined on this stone. "

The Bishop's Stone is said to be either haunted or, at the very least, 'inhabited' by a goblin, a rare occurrence in a landscape largely populated by pixies. It is said that at night grown men passing here were reduced to quivering wrecks, whilst by day horses refused to pass by without reacting violently. Cecil Torr believed that the explanation lay with a subterranean flow of water whose eerie noise scared both men and horses.

The Teign Naturalists were out in force at Lustleigh again in 1907 for another fieldwork visit:
"Leaving the village, a most romantic lane led through woods and fields to the Cleave, where the picnic was held near the Logan Rock. Here Mr and Mrs Hunt (Mr A. R. Hunt is a past president of the Club) joined, and conducted the party along the ridge to the Camp at the north end of the hill. From this point a most extensive and varied view was enjoyed of the whole wooded valley of the Bovey Brook, with the tors and moors around Manaton and North Bovey, and the distant elevation of Cosdon Beacon.

A business meeting was held here, the President (Mr R. Burnard, F.S.A.) in the chair, when the Secretary read the proceedings at the Annual Meeting which were confirmed.

Mr Hunt, then guided the Club down the steep hillside to his pleasant cottage at Foxworthy, where Mrs Hunt had invited the party to tea, which was found awaiting. After tea Mr Hunt read a valuable paper on Fernworthy and Lustleigh Cleave. There was a short discussion in which several members took part.

The return to Lustleigh Station, by Foxworthy Mill, and across the Cleave, among rocks and ferns, with the setting sun over the Manaton hills, was very charming, and made an appropriate conclusion to a pleasant day.

I had prepared a few notes on Rudge Farm, but as time did not permit our visiting it, they were not read. I give them now for the benefit of readers ... It appears that in removing the old farmhouse at Rudge in 1837, a primer of a singular character was found behind some wainscoting. It contains the alphabet, some columns of spelling, the Catechism, Graces to be said before and after meals and on retiring to rest ... This little book was bound in leather, having on one side a mermaid, and on the other Oliver Cromwell on horseback ... There is no date on the book ..."

Foxworthy Mill had been a working mill until 1878 and its last miller was Simon Martin. He was the proud owner of a donkey whose name was 'Black Jack'. Mr Hunt, referred to above, had bought the neglected mill in 1885 and had saved it from becoming a ruin. In the 1920s it was let to Farmer Leaman who had a dairy here.

'WPS' walked in the vicinity of Lustleigh almost a century ago and waxed lyrical about the countryside, which remains beautiful to this day: *"On a bright summer's morning in June 1907, I directed my course towards the vast solitudes of Dartmoor, and passing over romantic tracts of country beyond Dunsford Bridge, turned off from the vicinity of Moreton, in the parish of Hennock, which is most agreeably diversified with every variety of arable, water and coppice, and not the less renowned for its gigantic columns of basaltes, or the dense black gigantic elvan, at Bottor Rock, – the transition granite, greenstone (or woodstone, of the ungeological peasant;) from which, after a long ride through a number of tortuous but highly picturesque roads, slades, shaws, and lanes, I diverged to the left, towards the village lane of Lustleigh, and upward to that neat and time-hallowed edifice known as its (once a mansion house) rectory, seated on a tall eminence above the church, which overlooks a noble extent of country, far into the verdant basin or vale of Bovey Heathfield, and the sunny glades and waving woods of Ilsington and Ashburton.*

Nothing can be more interesting to the tourist than the 'shady brows' of the scenery afforded by the empurpled heath and luxuriant oak coppice which mantles the precipitous bluffs ... Lustleigh is noted for a grand rocking stone ... where the Bovey brook disappears among the jostling rocks of a miniature 'Sympleglades,' which abound with decorative lichens and rare plants, and for a noble cascade, known by the name of Becky Fall, to both of which a visit must be paid by the strolling tourist and by the frequent gay and picnic coteries of the ambrosial days

Around & About Lustleigh

of a Devonian summer ... The origin of the name might be 'the place of the camp on the water,' from the British 'Lhu,' a fort or camp, and 'Is' water ..."

William Crossing knew Lustleigh Cleave well and wrote this precise definition of it: *"The valley ... is formed by the ridge situated between the Wray and the Bovey, and the steeps rising from the latter to the farm land of Manaton. One side of it is bare common, the other is clothed with woods. At the lower end of the valley this further side takes the form of a peninsulated ridge, at the extremity of which the Bovey and Becka brook unite their waters. This is known as Hound Tor Ridge. On the further side of this ridge the Becky comes down from Hound Tor Combe, the valley here being formed by the wood and East Down, as the common below Trendlebere Down is called. N W of Sharp Tor is a rock called Harton Chest ... on the highest part of the ridge ... is the Lustleigh Camp. Quite near*

to it is Hunters Tor, from which the hill drops down to the enclosed lands at its N W extremity ... Not far from Hunters Tor is Peck Farm, a name borne by some old mining remains near by, these being usually known as Peck Pits."

The most famous rock outcrop in Lustleigh Cleave is the Nutcrackers which, as its name suggests, was once used to crack nuts, particularly at Christmas time. It was one of the best examples of a logan or logging stone. This type of feature was a granite block that was so delicately balanced on a fulcrum that the application of even relatively light weights to certain points could make it 'log' before resuming the same balanced position. The Nutcrackers could be rocked by a strong hand and its reputation was legendary in this district of Dartmoor. Of course care was needed to make sure that when this great rock was set in motion nobody's person was 'neath this great weight. Logan stones have a habit of losing their logging powers with overuse but this was not the case with the eight-ton Nutcrackers in Lustleigh Cleave. This report appeared on 11 May 1950: *"Dartmoor's famous Nutcracker Rock is no more. Someone has pushed it down into the valley below. It was so precariously balanced that it could be gently rocked by hand. The discovery was made yesterday when a villager looking up towards the heights above the village noticed that something was missing ... Mr F. Amery, clerk to the Lustleigh Parish Council, said that someone with crowbars must have levered the rock out of place. 'We should need a great deal of equipment to get the rock back into position. It is a sheer case of vandalism.'"*

The newspapers, both national and local, of June 1950 gave excellent coverage to the ill-fated efforts, and ultimately disastrous outcome, of those who set off with a mettlesome determination to rectify the sorry situation and put the rock back to its original logging position.

"Lustleigh Cleave's logan stone and landmark will be restored to its ancient site this afternoon providing the weather improves after yesterday's rain and there are no mishaps.

Major E. H. Graham, in charge of Plymouth Coast Artillery School's 'Operation Nutcracker' to raise the rock 40 feet to the base from which it was dislodged ... The 40 men engaged have made such good headway ... A number of the party will be National Service men, and the whole operation, led by Capt W. Juniper, is expected to arouse great local interest ... Villagers and holidaymakers climbed to the top of the cleave to watch the soldiers at work yesterday ... A 40 foot spar for raising the rock had been hoisted to the summit of a clump of rocks and six tons of equipment had been carried half a mile from the camp to the scene. Then heavy rain halted activity for the day.

A five inch hemp hawser which will take the weight of the rock remained in a tarpaulin covering because its use when wet or damp would be dangerous. If the weather is suitable today pulleys will be placed around the rock. A hand-worked winch will raise the stone, which will then be manoeuvred into position.

At present it rests against an oak tree and another boulder, which both holds it from rolling far down into the ravine and enables the sling to be placed in position.

Lustleigh will not be so much concerned if the 'Nutcracker' ceases to be a rocking stone so long as it occupies its old position commanding the valley. For years only a few 'in the know' could move it."

Alas, despite the best intentions of these conscripts the headlines from 20 June 1950 told a sad story: *"Nutcracker Rock 'too tough a nut to crack'."* The journalist must have had this headline cued up half-hoping to use it. *"Lustleigh Cleave's 'nutcracker' rock crashed 100 feet into the ravine yesterday, splitting against obstructing boulders as it fell, to put to an end for all time hopes that it would return to its old position.*

For a week troops had worked to raise it to the pedestal from which it was dislodged five weeks ago.

Awkwardly perched on the cliff face, they were striving to complete the turning of the rock on a narrow ledge on to which it had been eased from a supporting boulder and an oak tree. The overhanging rocking stone overbalanced and then slid off the ledge. Onlookers had been moved out of the danger zone.

Major Graham said, 'As the rock bounced down, hitting the cliff face, there was a thick cloud of sulphur-like fumes coming from it, and pieces flew off in every direction.'

Some 1,200 man hours have been worked by the 40 officers and men ... 'Still, it has been a first-class experience for the men and the hospitality of Lustleigh has been wonderful,' he said."

Lustleigh Cleave.

Under yet another headline *"Any Old Rock Is Not Good Enough"* a reporter with the pseudonym 'Junius' wrote: *"Certainly the half-dozen or so newspapermen representing national and Devon journals who made the daily pilgrimage to the Cleave to tell the tale for their readers bade the rock farewell with no regrets.*

With all the goodwill in the world one could not help becoming irritated with the Nutcracker that was always cutting through cables and making itself generally difficult to manipulate.

The suggestion has been made that the Army might put another boulder on the pedestal where the Nutcracker used to balance. It is an idea that does not commend itself to many Dartmoor-lovers. They take the view that Nutcracker had that extra something the others haven't got." There is a modern bungalow called Nutcracker at the nearby hamlet of Hammerslake.

A 1920s guide book referred to some of the other unusual rocks found in the same area: "Some quaint names of objects and places are to be found in the vicinity of the Cleave. The Round of Beef is difficult to carve and the Parson's Loaf or Brown Loaf more than hard on the teeth, but unless you have gone wrong when making a flying visit to the Nutcracker you will not be displeased when you find the Gate of Heaven."

In those halcyon days it was possible to take tea at Hammerslake, where there was a tea-room which did well out of the numerous walkers who came to explore Lustleigh Cleave.

'We Donkeys' on Dartmoor is an unusual title for a book but Maria Gibbons who published it in 1886 was no ordinary 'gal'! She lived, and is now buried, at East Budleigh in East Devon but in an active life she explored Devon in a small trap pulled by a pair of donkeys, the unusually-named 'Nem. Con.' and 'Xenophon Edward', hence the title. Where they couldn't go she explored on foot and this is an extract from her visit to the Lustleigh area. However, her geography of the district wasn't so good…

"We intended to cross the river – whether it be the Teign or Bovey Brook here we do not know – at Horsham Steps, but by mistake crossed it at the bridge at Foxworthy. However, we went down to the river again at Horsham Steps, which no sojourner in these parts should fail to visit. They form a natural bridge of granite boulders, under and between which the river roars and tumbles grandly. We also mistook our path a little after this by keeping too close to the river and thus getting very much into the bog – even to the extent of being thoroughly 'stogged' – but after this experience we learnt our mistake, and the only evil resulting from it was that we had to climb a stiffer part of the hill than we otherwise should. Here and elsewhere we found 'Badeley and Ward's Thorough Guides' most trustworthy as to routes and maps; but we think that the gentleman who took the 'Dartmoor section' was, at the time he wrote it, unfortunately suffering from indigestion. He certainly looked at things with a 'jaundiced eye.' His general description of Dartmoor does not tally with the feelings of those who know it best and therefore love it most, and his 'special' descriptions are greatly below the mark – for instance when he speaks of a church like Lustleigh as being 'without interest'.

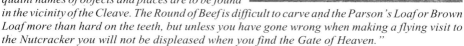

We reached the 'Nutcrackers' after a stiff pull up, in which – probably having got off the right path – hands as well as feet were requisite. We did not try the powers of the 'Logan Stone'; indeed, we don't think we could have reached it, but sitting down once or twice in the ascent, we looked across to our 'own' little cottage – a most commanding object on the other side of the valley – and saw very well, on that clear day, Bowerman's Nose, Saddle Tor, and Hey Tor; and we looked down at the 'Cleave', fresh in its luxurious spring foliage, which we had just left. After crossing the ridge of the hill, we descended for rather more than a mile to Lustleigh. Here, having obtained a good luncheon at the 'Cleave Hotel', we proceeded to the church dedicated to St John. The screen of this church is very beautiful, and has been remarkably well restored."

One of the children christened in the church's Norman font had Flood for his surname, something his family could do little about. However by christening their young one 'Noah' they opened up the proverbial flood gates for a torrent of good-natured ridicule – in Bovey Tracey he was bestowed with the nickname 'The Ark'.

Those who visit Lustleigh Cleave should enjoy the wonderful views afforded from the high points above the woods. It is a spectacular valley and is probably a better place for not having the hordes of 'trippers' that it hosted in the early part of the twentieth century. Some of them reported seeing the ghosts of Roman soldiers in the Cleave.

Close to Hunter's Tor, a high point above the Cleave, one may also see, in broad daylight, the ghosts of a party of phantom riders dressed in colourful hunting attire. Those who have witnessed this spooky spectacle have estimated that their costumes are from the fourteenth or fifteenth centuries. Their horses are beautifully caparisoned, that is decoratively covered by rich cloth. The fine horsemen have hawks on their wrists and are accompanied by their servants who scuttle along the Cleave on foot, dodging the dogs that run with them. However, just as your eyes begin to focus on this bizarre procession the whole entourage completely fades away!

Old picture postcards of Lustleigh Cleave also show mountain goats on rocky crags. The walkers exploring the Lustleigh district today may not see goats or ghosts but they will see much the same scenery as those of yesteryear. Ramblers will have to negotiate some physically, and sometimes mentally, 'challenging' obstructions in the forms of stiles, kissing gates, random rocks, raging rivers, slippery stones, half-hidden tree roots, cunningly-constructed clams and so on. But that is all part of the fun of walking and exploring the Lustleigh countryside, where there are such terrific moorland views to be had – for those who make the effort!